HISTORY OF FUN STUFF

The Deep Dish on Pizza!

by Stephen Krensky
illustrated by Daniel Guidera

Ready-to-Read

Simon Spotlight
New York   London   Toronto   Sydney   New Delhi

SIMON SPOTLIGHT

An imprint of Simon & Schuster Children's Publishing Division

1230 Avenue of the Americas, New York, New York 10020

This Simon Spotlight edition August 2014

For information about special discounts for bulk purchases, please contact Simon & Schuster Special
Sales at 1-866-506-1949 or business@simonandschuster.com.

The Simon & Schuster Speakers Bureau can bring authors to your live event. For more information or
to book an event contact the Simon & Schuster Speakers Bureau at 1-866-248-3049 or visit our website
at www.simonspeakers.com.

Manufactured in the United States of America 0621 LAK

4 6 8 10 9 7 5 3

Library of Congress Cataloging-in-Publication Data

The deep dish on pizza / by Stephen Krensky ; illustrated by Daniel Guidera.

pages cm. — (History of fun stuff) (Ready-to-read)

Includes bibliographical references and index.

Audience: Grades K–3.

ISBN 978-1-4814-2055-6 (trade paper) — ISBN 978-1-4814-2056-3 (hardcover) —
ISBN 978-1-4814-2057-0 (eBook) 1. Pizza—Juvenile literature. I. Guidera, Daniel, illustrator.

TX770.P58D42 2014

641.82'48—dc23

2013050058

CONTENTS

CHAPTER 1
The First Pizzas

If you stop to think about it, pizza may just be the perfect food. Of course, it helps that pizza can be different things to different people. Sure, you start with a crust made from dough. But is it thin or thick? You decide. Most people add tomato sauce and cheese, but what about toppings? Do you prefer pepperoni or mushrooms? What about onions or sausage? You choose again. And again. Sometimes the decisions are hard. And what if you want a pizza with everything?

When it comes to eating pizza, you may already know what you like. But what about the story behind what ends up in your mouth? Do you know who made the first pizza? Did ancient pizza look like the pizza we eat today? Or has it changed over the years? That's where this book comes in.

By the time you finish it, you'll know the answers to these questions and a lot more. You will be a History of Fun Stuff Expert on pizza!

We think of pizza as an Italian food. And the word "pizza" means "pie" in Italian. But is pizza really from Italy? We know that people were eating pizza in Italian cities like Pompeii more than two thousand years ago. (Unfortunately, Pompeii was destroyed by a volcanic explosion in AD 79. Nobody ate pizza there for a long time after that.) But believe it or not, pizza was actually born somewhere else!

9

Centuries earlier, the Greeks and
Phoenicians mixed flour and water to
make a simple dough for flatbread. They
seasoned it with herbs and cooked the
dough on a hot stone. (By the way, the

ancient Egyptians get the credit for adding yeast to bread, which made it rise up and easier to chew.) They called it *plankuntos,* and it wasn't really meant to be eaten by itself. Instead it was used as a kind of edible plate for stews or broth. This flatbread meal is generally considered to be the earliest form of pizza.

As far as toppings go, these early pizzas didn't have much on them. However, they were handy meals for anyone on the move. The Persian emperor Darius the Great (550–486 BC) conquered a vast area from Greece to India. Nobody gives pizza the

GREECE

INDIA

Dates

credit for Persia's victories, but we know that Persian soldiers baked flatbread on their shields and topped it with cheese and dates. So eating pizza didn't hurt.

CHAPTER 2
Pizza on the Rise

Pizza may have started in the countries around the Mediterranean Sea, but one of its key ingredients, the tomato, came from about 7,000 miles away. Tomatoes are native to the Americas. The first tomato seeds only arrived in Europe in the 1500s. Its first prominent mention came in the 1550s, when it became known as the *pomi d'oro*, the "golden apple."

"Golden apple" sounds like a nice name, but tomatoes were not received with open arms. Some people were suspicious of them because they were bright and shiny and grew so close to the ground. Other people became sick after eating them. The rumor that they were poisonous lasted for centuries. It turned out that the acid

in the tomato sometimes combined with the pewter in pewter plates—which was what made people sick. By the end of the 1800s, pewter was no longer used much for plates, so eating tomatoes was no longer a problem. Now they were ready to take their proper place in the kitchen.

Even after people wanted to make pizza, there was still the problem of cooking it. In the late 1700s, the Queen of Naples, Maria Carolina, could afford to have a special oven built at her summer palace so that pizza could be served to her guests.

Her poorer subjects were not as fortunate. Ovens were expensive, and most Italian villagers didn't have one. So they shared a town oven, using it to bake pizza and bread.

Pizza was popular for two important reasons. The first was that it tasted good. The second was that it was cheap. Street vendors kept the price down by cutting up the pizzas and selling them one slice at a time. For people who wanted to eat sitting down, the first pizzeria opened in Naples around 1830. It had a wood-fired brick-lined oven. The place was popular, and soon

Naples was filled with pizzerias. Most of
the pizzas sold there were made in the
marinara style. They were simply topped
with tomato, garlic, oregano, and olive oil.
It was called "marinara," the name for a
seaman's wife. Why? Because fishermen's
wives often prepared the dish for their
husbands to eat when they returned home.

You would think that people who didn't like pizza would just skip it and move on. But, no, some of them had to make their opinions known. Samuel Morse, an American who was most famous for inventing the telegraph, made his opinion clear. Pizza, he said while visiting Naples in the 1830s, was a nauseating cake. It was "covered with slices of pomodoro or tomatoes, and sprinkled with little fish and black pepper and I know not what other ingredients, it altogether looks like a piece of bread that had been taken reeking out of the sewer."

Even some Italians were not pizza fans. Carlos Collodi, the author of *The Adventures of Pinocchio*, said in the 1800s that the toppings of garlic, fried herbs, and bits of tomato gave pizza "the appearance of complicated filth that matches the dirt of the vendor." Now that doesn't sound very appealing, does it?

But these naysayers were in the minority. Pizza was becoming more popular than ever. In 1889 the Italian king Umberto I and his wife, Queen Margherita, visited Naples. Among its popular restaurants was the Pizzeria di Pietro, owned by Raffaele Esposito. It is said that in honor of the royal visit, Esposito made three pizzas for the queen. Two were already well-known

recipes, but the third—which combined mozzarella cheese, basil, and tomatoes— was something new. Together, the three ingredients matched the white, green, and red of the Italian flag. The queen reportedly loved her pizza so much that Esposito decided to name it after her. That's why we call it the pizza margherita.

CHAPTER 3
Spreading the Word

America had sent tomatoes to Europe back in the 1500s, but it took almost four hundred years before Europe returned the favor. In the early 1900s, many immigrants came to the United States looking for work. Among the thousands arriving from southern Italy was Gennaro Lombardi. In 1905 he opened the first American pizzeria in New York City. It was a good beginning. Still, the only people eating pizza were the ones who had come from Italy themselves or whose parents had made the trip. What changed to make pizza catch on and become a beloved food in the USA?

Nearly forty years after the first pizzeria opened in New York, many American soldiers spent considerable time in Italy during World War II. The army fed them, of course . . . but when you were facing a constant diet of food that started out powdered or came out of tins (or both), it was tempting to look around for alternatives. One of these options was pizza. It was simple, it was fast, and everyone from privates to four-star generals brought their taste for it back home after the war ended.

When it came to serving pizza to all those returning soldiers, there weren't enough Gennaro Lombardis to go around, so the demand for more pizza options kept growing. In response, Ike Sewell opened the deep-crusted Pizzeria Uno in Chicago in 1943, and in the 1950s, pizza chains appeared. Shakey's Pizza was the first. It opened in Sacramento,

California, in 1954. Further east, in Wichita, Kansas, Pizza Hut opened its doors in 1958. In the years that followed, Little Caesar's, Domino's, Papa John's, and California Pizza Kitchen, among others, made their debuts. Have you ever enjoyed a slice from any of these places?

One of the best things about pizza is that it can also be enjoyed at home! Delivery is one popular option, but that isn't always convenient. For people who wanted to enjoy pizza at home but didn't want to have it delivered, Rose Totino had a solution. In 1962 she started Totino's Finer Foods, which produced frozen pizzas that could be baked at home. Although the business was successful from the beginning, Rose Totino spent more than sixteen years perfecting the recipe for the crust. Today there are aisles in the supermarket dedicated to many varieties of frozen pizzas.

But frozen pizza isn't for everyone. In
the 1980s, much fancier pizzas began to
appear. They were not for sale in your
average pizzeria, though. The famous chef
Wolfgang Puck pioneered gourmet pizzas at
his restaurant Spago in Los Angeles. These

pizzas were topped with exotic things like truffles and caviar. In fact, perhaps the most expensive pizza ever made boasted among its ingredients edible flecks of real gold. What is the most exotic pizza topping you've ever tried?

CHAPTER 4
Pizza Conquers the World

As a love of pizza has spread all over the world, new variations keep turning up. A popular pizza pie in Japan is made with a combination of mayonnaise, potato, and bacon on top. In India, pickled ginger is a favorite topping. Brazilians will put all kinds of things—from hard-boiled eggs to hearts of palm—on a soft crust.

One way or another, whether eating out or eating at home, Americans swallow a lot of pizza. 94 percent of us eat pizza regularly, averaging about seven and one-half pizzas a year. That's about 350 slices of pizza per second, enough to cover almost one hundred acres every day! And a little more than a third of those acres are covered with pepperoni, America's favorite topping. (So if you haven't been eating your share of pizza, now's the time to catch up!)

Congratulations! You've come to the end of this book. Assuming you didn't just skip to this page to see how things turned out, you are now an official History of Fun Stuff Expert on pizza. Go ahead and impress your friends and family with all the cool stuff you've learned about one of the world's most popular foods. But use your power wisely. And the next time you order a slice of pizza, remember it comes from a long and proud tradition. And then take a really big bite!

Hey, kids! Now that you're an expert on the history of pizza, turn the page to learn even more about it and some geography, science, and geometry along the way!

41

The Geography of Italy

Italy may be famous for its pizza, but there's much more to explore! Learn about the geography of Italy below.

Italy is a boot-shaped peninsula in the Mediterranean Sea. A **peninsula** is a body of land that is surrounded by water on three sides. The state of Florida is a peninsula too! Can you think of any other famous peninsulas?

Italy's mainland is covered with mountains, including the Dolomite Mountains in northern Italy and the Apennine Mountains in the center of the country. A **mountain** is a very tall piece of land (at least one thousand feet high) with steep slopes and a point called a peak.

Dolomite Mts.

ITALY

Sardinia

Apennine Mts.

Sicily

The islands of Sicily and Sardinia are also part of Italy. An **island** is a body of land that is smaller than a continent and is surrounded by water on all sides (unlike a peninsula, which is surrounded by water on three sides. . . . Right, geography expert?).

Sardinia is a rocky island where about 1.5 million people live, while Sicily is home to more than five million people. Sardinia and Sicily are very big—each is nearly ten thousand square miles! That's more than twice the size of Hawaii's biggest island!

Mamma mia! Now you know all about the geography of Italy!

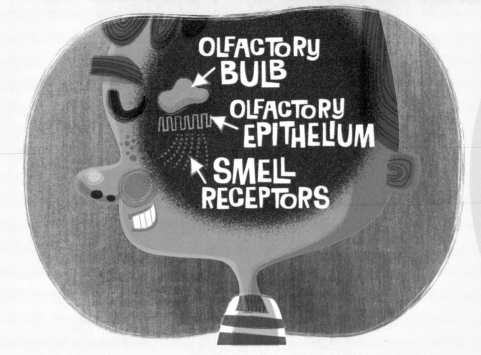

Your Nose Knows! The Power of Smell

When you walk into a pizza parlor, what is the first thing you notice? The delicious smell of pizza, of course! But how does our sense of smell work?

Inside the space behind your nose is the **olfactory epithelium** [ol·FAK·tah·ree eh·puh·THEE·lee·um]. The **olfactory epithelium** has special **smell receptors** that react to different kinds of smells. And there are lots of different kinds of smells—your nose has about ten million receptors!

When the receptors react to a smell, a signal travels to the **olfactory bulb**, located under the front of your brain. From there, the signal is sent to different parts of your brain to be interpreted. Is that the delicious smell of pizza cooking in the oven, or the smell of pizza burning in the oven?

Speaking of which, why does pizza smell best when it comes out of the oven? When you smell something, teeny tiny particles of pizza, called molecules, have to travel up into your nose. These odor molecules set off the different receptors in your nose, telling your brain that . . . it's dinnertime!

How Many Ways
Can You Slice a Pizza?

If you're really, *really* hungry, you could possibly eat a whole pizza, but normally you cut it up and share it with friends.

When you split one thing into equal pieces, you  can represent this by using a **fraction**. Below, you can use a **fraction** to represent your share of the pizza (the numerator on the top) over the total slices of pizza (the denominator on the bottom).

Let's say you want to share your pizza with just one friend. You could cut the pizza into **halves**. When you split one thing into two equal pieces, you split it in **half**. The fraction for one half is 1 (your slice) / 2 (total number of slices).

1/2

1/3

Or you could invite another friend over, and slice the pizza into **thirds**. You get a **third** when you split one thing into three equal pieces. The fraction for one third is 1 (your slice) / 3 (total number of slices).

Or if you invite one more person over, you can cut the pizza into **quarters**. You get a **quarter** when you split one thing into four equal pieces. The fraction for one quarter is 1 (your slice) / 4 (total number of slices).

1/4

Being an expert on something means you can get an awesome score on a quiz on that subject! Take this

HISTORY OF PIZZA QUIZ

to see how much you've learned.

1. *Plankuntos*, an early form of pizza, was actually used as an edible plate to hold what?

   a. Candy   b. Stews or broth   c. Ice cream

2. What did Darius the Great's Persian soldiers bake their flatbread on?

   a. Swords   b. Spears   c. Shields

3. In the 1500s, many Europeans believed tomatoes were _____.

   a. Poisonous   b. Tasty   c. Purple

4. Around what year did the first pizzeria open in Naples?

   a. 1910   b. 1340   c. 1830

5. What is pizza margherita named after?

   a. A town in Italy   b. Queen Margherita   c. A type of flower

6. Which type of pizza was invented first?

   a. *Plankuntos*   b. Chicago Deep Dish   c. Pizza margherita

7. Gennaro Lombardi opened the first American pizzeria in which city?

   a. Chicago   b. New York City   c. Minneapolis

8. Pizza became popular in America immediately after _____.

   a. The Civil War   b. The sinking of the Titanic   c. World War II

9. Who invented frozen pizzas in 1962?

   a. Wolfgang Puck   b. Rose Totino   c. Maria Carolina

10. Americans eat enough pizza to cover almost ____ acres each day.

    a. one hundred   b. one million   c. twenty-three

Answers: 1. b   2. c   3. a   4. c   5. b   6. a   7. b   8. c   9. b   10. a